Dear Mari,
Thank you
so much

THE DARK CAVE
BETWEEN MY RIBS

for EVERYTHING!

Loren Kleinman

you are just
an inspiration
+ a SUPERSTAR!

Winter Goose
Publishing

Winter Goose Publishing
2701 Del Paso Road, 130-92
Sacramento, CA 95835

www.wintergoosepublishing.com
Contact Information: info@wintergoosepublishing.com

The Dark Cave Between My Ribs

COPYRIGHT © 2014 by Loren Kleinman

First Edition, March 2014

ISBN: 978-1-941058-06-0

Cover Painting by Herlander Passos
Cover Art by Winter Goose Publishing
Typeset by Odyssey Books

Published in the United States of America

I want
my heart back
I want to feel everything again
—Louise Glück

Table of Contents

I

The Window I Sleep By

The night opens up my chest:
poems come out
of the dark cave
between my ribs.

I can't see what is written,
maybe I'm too scared to face it,
I'm too scared.

I close my eyes,
and see a mountain
in the doorway.

I've never felt more alone
in a world that tells me
you're not alone.

I'm silent
and the room becomes
the small window I sleep by.

When I can't sleep,
I look out the window
and imagine I'm loved.

If I had love,
I would name it an infinite name.

If I had love
I would speak its language.

If *I* were only mine,
I'd be floating in space, glittering
and disfigured.

If only I could tell you my past,
but I'm humiliated to say
I only listen.

Suppose my past did this to me:
made me afraid of love.

Why can't I cry?

I don't know,
says the body.

Remembering My Grandmother

My grandmother's hands drip olive oil and salt.

She begins to dip
strips of codfish into beer batter,
and drapes the fish in the heated oil.

The food always tastes different here.

I watch the way her hands cup
the fragile fish,
how she spreads the egg yolk
across its skin,
so thin.

Everything is cared for.
Everything in its place.

I try to listen to the smells,
the years of preparing and tasting,
drinking the cellar wine.

I wonder if I'll sense time
and texture:
the way salt is spared in some dishes
and how it is produced for others.

Tonight, I watch her move
the wooden spoon with her fingers,
an expert, turning it
in complete circles.

She picks up some sauce,
holds it to her lips,
and breathes in and out.

More onion, she hums.

She will leave me with the cutting board,
the mahogany table in the dining room,
her old-world porcelain,
leave me to unstring the stuffed meats,
scrape the seeds
from a burst cantaloupe.

I will have to glaze the Christmas Struffala with honey,
and make the bread,
at Easter, rise.

Somehow, I'll know what to do:
touch the skin of this world.

Peel it back.

I Wanted to Be the Echo of the World

I break in the porcelain of your hands.

I wanted to tell you
that I've been raped.
He took everything I had
and broke it
with his puckered skin.

I wanted to die,
to die.

The only thing that saved me
was my mother's voice.

Yesterday I got a tattoo—
it hurt less than your porcelain hands.

I'm shaking,
breaking
in a sea of glass.

All my love is gone.
Gone.

The walls never come up
because they are gone.

The walls never come up because they are painted
dark, strange colors.

Today I'll drive to the hospital
and think about the echo
I wanted to be in the world,
think about your hands
with me breaking in them.

I finally fall apart.

I miss the world sometimes,
and my grandpa and myself
and my mom.

I miss being a kid
playing in the backyard,
kicking up dirt
and smiling
and eating candy.

When did I grow up?

When did it all happen
without anyone telling me?

If I could give this feeling a name
I would,
but you wouldn't fall in love with me.

Today I glue myself back together.

In your hands,
I'm the porcelain echo.

He Couldn't Stop

Leave my body alone,
I said.

Why is it happening
all over again?

This isn't me
or my future.

What did his skin feel like?

I'm broken winged,
a fallen bird on the black road.

And why hasn't anyone helped you?

I'm swimming in the harmless
shadow,

the light, the light,
swimming.

What did the light taste like?

Metallic poison.

How did you get rid of it?

He couldn't stop.
Hard

and stunned drunk,
he ripped
through panty hose.

How did it feel?

Millions of bees stinging
between my thighs.

And this is your life?

Wine and breeze condemn me,
gradually.

Don't turn around?

Don't turn around.

A Great Fall

I woke up broken,
my arms, legs, fingers, toes,
hair and teeth scattered
on the floor,
the wooden planks piled
with bone and vessels
running into each other,
making knots
and neckties
out of fleshy organs
and fingernails plucked,
flowers from the beds
of puffy skin,
wasted and pecked
from the shell
of the torso,
wobbling around,
searching over the floor
for the dislocated parts
breathing
breathing
making a skin basket
to carry
the missing pieces,
try to put them back,
put them back
together.

I'm Stuck in My Dream

Stuck in a dream:
In a building with no exit.
In the middle of the street
caught between moving cars.
Walking over pregnant bellies
poking through the muddy ground.
Wearing the same shoes
I've been wearing
in the same dream from last night.

I see my eight-year-old self,
bleeding behind the broken
chair in my old room.
My mother walks around drunk.
She points knives into my skin,
and dies too fast.

Fast-forward to thirty.
Making love to you in my mind—
so lovely,
I kiss my own hand like it's your mouth
pressing into my tongue.

Stuck in a dream,
never getting it right.
Running far away.
Hiding on a dream cloud.
Sleeping in my bed.
Carried away.
Sticking it out in all the wrong ways.

Breaking down.
Walking.
Faking it.

Wondering what it would be like
being found dead in my bathtub.

Death,
not so scary.

Stuck in a dream,
writing a suicide letter.
Starting it
and still thinking
about what to do later.
You'll forget about me.

Back to beginning.

Belonging to you.
Laughing hard at all your jokes.
If you love me,
you'll notice me.

Losing you in my thoughts
under the painted ceiling
of my bedroom.

Terrified.
Eyes crying
all over me.

Look.
At.
Me.

Smiling at you.

Stay and Listen

For Franz Wright

Behind the fog,
one gull flies
over the North Sea,

a ghost
entering in place of words,
among all these thoughts
of death.

Something here wants you
to love.

II

Dumb Drunk Love Poem

I wanted to tell you
I always want to die.
I want to die into the crook
where your arm meets your shoulder.

Where do I go now, love?
How do I come back from lost love?
Why did you leave me stranded
on my apartment floor drinking Vermouth
and my life away?

I never love myself
like I tell you I love myself.
I never show you my greatest fear
is ending up like my mother: a drunk.

Every minute I make mistakes.

I own them,
and I get lost
in the keyboard of my computer.

I don't mean to get drunk,
but I am right now.

I'm so drunk
and write this dumb
love poem, waiting
and hoping

you'll take me back.

Everything Must Go

Everything must go
so you buy one thing,
a pencil sharpener.

You read a poem.
You are the poem.
You wish you wrote the poem.
Bukowski laughs at your envy.

Long silence.

Words,
unbearable.

You go out for dinner.

Get the soup,
someone says.
It was Bukowski's favorite.

Every Moment I'm Not All Right

Life is a whisper.
I'm lonely. I can't sleep.

One day it will be another century.
I'm going there, but I don't know if I'll be happy.

What's over there? Transformation? Reform?
I was raped. He held me down.

Not even a glacier could hold me on the sea.
What was I born for?

Something passes within me.
I can hear my widowed dreams coming back.

Every moment I'm not all right.
Who will remember that I was cut?

Who will remember that I said *no?*
Did I mean it?

The Devil's Breath

1.

A burnt figure
in the well
of dreams

shook out
the devil's breath

and took my voice.

2.

In the center
of my stomach
sits a storehouse of all things
anxiety-ridden, and full

of tiny fish
laying their eggs alongside

my muddy bowels.

3.

I'm a casualty of memory,
she said.

Silence
is a familiar language

like his hands,
large and rough with scabs,

dry skin, cracked
and reptilian.

4.

I couldn't save my body,
she said,

held in the place
of no light,

hidden.

5.

I thought I was safe,
she said.

And were his hands quiet?

Not in the end.

I Forgot to Tell You

Even in our long talks
I leave things out.

I could tell you when he took me to the bathroom
angels spoke to me:
Go inside—

They abandoned me.

The Consequences of Cutting

There was nothing left to save.

My body became a fossil
coiled on the floor.

In the end
the skin still bled.

My consequence was hooked
in an emergency room
somewhere
on the precipice of death.

Something looked
at me

with its soft,
feathery face,

holding out its wings,
and asked

for the dreams
that cut me.

Ode to Finding Happiness

I bear no resemblance to life,
to the trees and mint and the grapes.

The world is spaced out
on highways and sideways,

under the dirt in my fingernails,
and concrete foundations under houses,

and the parts in stories left out,
and the hellos spaced out between years
and years and years,
and in the repetition of life.

I wish I could find the happiness
that I read about in books
that exists in deep breathing and meditation.

I've looked under the blanket
where I've hidden my head
in shame,

away from the possibility of love and intimacy,
from the alcoholism in my family
away from the chance that I may be a drunk

alone and drunk and alone—

Happiness would be great.

It could open me up to more happiness,
but I'm not sure what would help,
and I don't want to try yoga or smiling,
or force myself to look on the bright side of everything.

Where are you, smile?
Where are you, laughter?

Oh, I'll wait around like a fool
for you to take my hand
and walk me away from the bright edge,

the sun melting away my anger,
growing the seeds for a new life.

I Want No Paradise

This is how life looks
when it's turning into nothing,
nothing at all,

a monument to cherish,
splintered driftwood,
drifting.

This is how the body erodes,
a condition of existence.

Why do I have to be here,
to see this,

to watch mass,
weight hang,
shadowed?

The body holds together
like some artifact,
or some big fish
stuck in the shallows,
showing itself:
bright stomach, raw eyes,
terrified.

This is when the bones
scrape against each other,
when they touch
in the heat of it all,
immersed
in the promise of death.

If I Were to Write a Suicide Note I Would Tell You

After years of therapy and pills,
nothing has made the difference.

The plums in the icebox have not made me want
to eat them more.

My grandfather's dialysis is not working.
My mother's alcoholism
makes me love her less.

In my head, the music is never off.

The man I'm dating now doesn't complete me.

I'd tell you that my friends think I'm strong,
and at night I go home and cry
and cut myself

and wish that for one second
I could forget
Man's Concern with Death

and fall in love
in my mother's arms again.

You Were Not Made for the World

You were not born for the world,
or modern life.

Rejection,
the most important lesson.

When he took me from you,
I couldn't remember my place,
in the dead skin we called our own.

I looked at you
when you were dying,

even when you thought
I wasn't looking,

even when you didn't want me
to look.

My God

I cannot carry it.
I cannot carry it.
If I could carry it,
I would carry it.

With mourning comes an unsayable pain.

I'm in a room somewhere,
a woman waiting to come back
as a woman.

My own name
is a stranger to me,

even my own death,
spread on the narrow bed.

Where were *You* when I was alone
and wanted to turn my sadness
into a religion?

I cannot carry this head.
I cannot carry this all
in my head.

If I could,
I would carry it across the continent

for the love of living
only you know,
can only carry it,
listening,
next to the bleached Broadway lights,

as the distance between us
disappears.

Sleep Song

It is night.
I hear your voice.

III

Good Sleeping Weather

The world gives itself away
in small whispers:
fresh prints in the mud
and a crocus mouth,
half-opened,
frozen.

The clouds,
a pile of wet towels.

I read, bent over the table
in the windy room,
All the constituents of being are Transitory.

I hope I'll see you again
in the secret place
where we loved each other.

It existed.
I think it existed.

It's Been Done Before

Look,
there are ghosts behind
the curtains.

A girl walks to the store
and gets hit by a car.
Her sneakers across from each other
on 5th Avenue.

People disappear.

It could've been you.
Thank God it wasn't you.

Your mother is drunk.
She makes coconut shrimp
but leaves them in the oven.
Dinner. Burnt.
Still hungry.

Poems get thrown in the trash,
old tennis shoes,
Band-Aids,
used tissue,
phone numbers on napkins.

You can't remember what day it is,
how old you are,
or what you ate for lunch.
Fish.

Somewhere it's night.
It's noon.
It's night again.

Someone says,
It looks like rain.

America, the Beautiful

This is America,
the dark house of fiction,
the dark horse,
the battle ground.

This is the place
where I danced
with my mother
in the den
before she was drunk
and chose wine
over her daughter.

This state, NJ,
is where I grew up
and lived for thirty years
in a home full of love,
drunk love
and non love.

Mother,
my mother,
she's her own country,

her borders closed,
highways full of inspectors,
streets turning
and winding with detours,
all under construction.

I miss her.

I wish she'd give up appearances,
the beer, the white wine,
the red wine,
how it makes her foreign,
the other reality,
shiny with red drunk cheeks.

I remember loving her once
in long sober hugs.

This is my song for her:
my mother,
my mother,
the beautiful.

My Grandfather is Dead

I am writing to you because I'm hoping
you watch my back.

When it all comes to me, I want you to know
that I am thinking of you.

I want you to know that I know
in this dream everything is you.
This evening I listen
and speak back to you in softness
and oldness.

The letters have small curves,
sharp points,
and dots,
and notations
that make up my story to you,

the story of us,

how our blood is single
and everlasting
in its dampness
and dialysis.

I wanted to write to you
because we can't speak any other way.

In the end
there is only whiteness,

everything new again.
In the end there is you
and family

and the haunting shape of kindness
to take you home.

In This Dark City I Don't Miss You At All

In this dark city
I don't miss you at all.

I don't think of your smile
or your smell.

In this dark night,
outside my window,

you don't haunt me.

I think of who I am,
of who I want to be
without you.

Without your hands to hold,
I don't miss you at all.

I don't think of your eyes
through rain and lights.

I don't miss you at all.

Fragments of Love

Wondering again
about love,

the fragments it leaves behind:

coffee cups,
books,
pictures.

Today, I think of the possibilities
of letting go,

the face I loved,

the only memory
never found,

a lost child
inside my body,

looking for peace.

The Shunned Angel

For H.D.

Take down the walls of the old church
and steal the candle,
the script,
and the bell.

Collect the fragments
of the body
and the blood.

Drink the wine,
the fire of breath,
and melt the wax from the candle
that stands on the pulpit
of the orator's podium,
where fractured bones of Jesus
hang on the cross
and turn from death to birth.

Watch as the world
gives up sand and shell
and sets fire to the beach
where so many stood
watching with their eyes
the water shaking out Titans.

The skies shun their angels
who chose to lie splintered in caves,
the others cast out by thunderbolt
into rocks or in a star
or in hearts.

Surrounded by a drift of wings,
the new sky steps out for the first time
into the magic of the atmosphere.

I'm Your Hostage

Tell me you want me to die.

Tell me these days
are fruitless and empty,

that I'm late for my life.

Life becomes what I want,
but the world has new plans,

it makes me crazy and psychotic
under the peeled, leaky ceiling
in my apartment.

It's hard to say
who I wanted to become
when I was young
and inexperienced,

or when I was playing
with my rock collection
in the backyard.

And when I'm caught,
held hostage
by the violence of my past,
I allow myself to die.

When the bullet hits,
I let it lodge between the stones
I hid right here
in the dirt of the heart.

Even when I'm wide open,
life,

stay.

Ghosts in Love

A pastiche for Julia Hartwig

We saw it one time
foggy and soft,
floating there,

calling
to us in the night—
love me.

We were wondering about falling in love.
That one day we may have to die into it.

We loved already.

We were thinking the moment of end will come soon.

Meanwhile, our friends,
our jobs,
our families would sink
to the bottom of the seas,
and become unrecognizable.

Starting tomorrow we will really love,
we said.

But this is already love,
and some of us have died for good.

Three Days After Your Death

For Ripley

I dreamt you were back in my arms.

The memory of you was blurred and light,
long as the highways.

I walked over to you,
and spoke in dead speak.

Your face looked like steel
blotted with mud.

Our eyes met in the darkness.

We faced the grass together.

We were home,
an abstract movement, intestinal—

swimming in slate banks,
broken and gouged
through metal crosses and ghosts.

But I couldn't reach you.

Your face was rotting beneath the water.
You were incomplete,
a snapshot of life caught in the grate,
a spark.

In this dream you came to me,
or maybe I came back to myself.

I saw you as torn pieces of flesh
trying to come back together.

I wanted to tell you,
live inside my head,
don't go.

But you ran out
and the orange sky widened, endless.

We Are Not Who We Thought We'd Be

We thought love
would make us whole.

We thought that with so much love
we'd be parked,
not searching anymore.

We believed that love
would bring us out of the darkness
face-to-face,

but we were pushed back
to the beginning,

the time we fell into the lit tunnels
of our souls.

Now we are trying to forget love
as if that would give us satisfaction.

We still don't hope
the other would fill the spaces
between our fingers.

My Body Opens

A tulip blooms
between my breasts.

A petal
shaky and falling
from the wind
glitters like a star
under my nipple.

My body closes
after the flower blooms,
stitches itself up
down the middle
of my torso.

A smudge of blood
at the seam.

A fingerprint
and a petal.

Memory, Like a Washing Machine

I imagine you here
in the secret place,
the whirl
of my memory
like a washing machine.

I'm hanging from the ceiling,
a chandelier.

The thought of our past
tortures me,
reminds me
you're-not-here,
you're-not-ever-coming-back,
ever, never.

Fossilized love,
I'm a human water board.

A waterfall forces me to the bottom
of a sandy ravine,
fish nibbling at my toes,

the water, shining
like grief.

I swim to get away,
to live without you
one day,
the day after
and fifty thousand years later.

When He Leaves Me Again

A desert opens in my room.

I reach out to touch him,
but I'm pricked by a cactus.

I shrink to tumbleweed
and roll away.

The world slows down around me,
and I reach out to the air,
the leaves,
the trees.

I brush the dust from my face
and watch tiny fire ants
lift him from our bed.

Where are they taking him?
Up? Down?
Over there?

As he floats through the air,
he's still under the blankets,
pillow under his head.

It's quiet now,
only the faint sound of his voice
guides me
through the dry roses.

Our Story

For Arek

It was fiction,
character sketches,
and drafts that weren't very good.

Was there time
to write the plot?

One more page goes by
despite you,
and the words don't
mean much.

The sentences are not real.

I've been writing our story a long time,
hard to tell how long.

If we were to rely on words,
I, love, you,
survive on them,

our hearts would open,

not wanting anything less
than what we've imagined.

How to Begin Again

The soul peeks out behind the skin,
like a game children play.

Sometimes it hides
without me knowing,
and when I look for it,
it runs away,

turns up the stairs
and under the bed.

I can hear it moving in the dark,
and the sound it makes.

When it appears
from beneath the bed frame,
it looks different,
defeated.

I found you, I say.

For a short moment
we stare at each other
like stabbed crows.

How do we begin again?

Prayer for Love

Take me, Lord.
Hold me against the halo
around your heart.

Lord, let me laugh.

For once,
let me be myself
and see the end of the world
through my eyelids.

Let the storm,
the apocalypse
come,
come.

Hold me, Lord.
Love me in your light.

When you let me go,
flood me with your blue ocean.

Oh Lord,
my mouth is open.

Pour the water in.

To My Past

Let my heart be free.

I don't want you anymore.

You're not
the whole world.

IV

The School with No Name

For the children of the Beslan school siege

The survivors couldn't forget the feel
of bodies beneath their bare feet
as they escaped.

The children left inside offer money,
but die thirsty.

Outside, the mothers curse the teachers
for leaving them.

The lucky ones were shot and killed.

Those left running
fall onto the flesh
of the ones who ran before them.

In a hallway, a *Shahidka* bursts
like a balloon
when she explodes.

Three hundred small bodies
in the gymnasium,

the ones who used to walk to school
holding their mothers' hands,

the ones who argued
over the last rubber ball,
kicking up dirt,

now they hold parts
of their skin together,
negotiate their lives.

I can't even imagine
the last thing children think of
when they know they are going to die.

Maybe their mother,
life before today,
the way certain things make them laugh
and they don't know why.

The way they are scared of the dark.

How in the beginning,
they were just the child,
pulling the note from the lunch bag,
which began, "Dear firefly,"

The Road

My death
will become lost

in the box
I'm buried in.

I won't be a girl
anymore.

I will belong
to the earth:

berries that fall
to the ground,

a slow,
fall breeze,

or dust
on the road.

I Came From the Earth

I came from the past,
dropped on the earth
somewhere deep in the woods,
maybe a forest or a creek,
a tiny spore floating
in the air across the lines
of branches stretching out
off from peeling trunks.

I started in the present,
alone and destitute
on a road somewhere
over there where the world
dropped me and then left me,
unwanted and sticky like sandspur.

In the future I became myself
abstract and metaphysical,
unknown, sort-of recognizable
a reflection of my non-face.

I'm neither in the past nor part
of the present, never
in the future,
closed off and dark.

You can find me,
brown eyes under lids,
lips peeled, skin cracked
beneath the under of my skin

in that somewhere I thought I knew,
pale and shallow of thought,
broken from the earth.

Writing to You, Forever and Ever

For Jack and Ina Polak

I see your face in the words I write,

in piles of shoes
and torn clothes,

in faces that died,
in the naked, toothless bodies
disinherited from the world,

in the dirt,
between wire and barb,

through the days,
weeks,
months,
years,

the long list of names
the guards call out to us,

in the void of ribs,
the reaper of love,
non-existent love,

in the suspension of death,

in our exile,
in names no longer mentioned,

in violence,
in all this doubt and crying,

in the soup,
in the holes in fences,

in my urgent fingers
writing.

They Want You to Believe it Never Happened in the Ponary Forest

Holding hands, they were shot one by one
and fell naked
into the fuel pits.

Only the young children
broke the hearts of soldiers
again and again
as they accepted firing.

Morning will come,
temporarily through the trees,
and assimilate the past.

Outside the forest,
the rest of Europe
is in the middle of dinner.

Łomza

In Łomza
you brush the dirt
off your mother's name.

It's the three of us.
One no longer needed.

We come back to this absurd village
to feel the world without her.

It looks like snow.

The cold makes it harder to breathe,
harder to remember where we're going.

Winter is hard,
and makes everything harder,
the fingers, the ground, the cabbage.

Can she forgive me for wanting
all of her son's love?

It's not enough,
and now I know it.

There are no people in Łomza
to miss you.

You Remember Your Mother's Suicide

Would she appear
if you stopped crying?

Would you see her cracked lips,
swollen eyes,
or her blue bandana wrapped around her head?

You blame yourself
for not bearing witness
to the mystery of her death.

You can hear her shaking
the puddles on the sidewalk
with her loud laugh.

Between your breath
and your arms and legs,

she passes like the cold
in the middle of winter
and never looks back at you.

And it does you no good
to hold out your arms in the night.

She wouldn't recognize you,
she wouldn't decide to return to ease your pain.

What about me,
you cry.

It's a mistake
to fall asleep and hope
that in the morning
you'd catch her folding your shirts,
or opening the shades,

letting the light in.

Left Behind in Times of War

This time I was lucky.

There was no wildness,
no despair,

no corpse gardens.

So what if I was born
a fragment,
thrown into a trash heap,
or shot roadside?

I never entered that door.
I wasn't the dead walking.

Someone is Dying Somewhere

Someone is dying somewhere.

Every minute
someone says I miss you,
I wish you were here.

In the past,
there is another past
waiting to come back,
clean and un-sick,

under the great silence
and dispersed atoms
of this world,

under the ugliness
and destruction.

I'm a Door

I'm a door,
hungry and dreaming,
the opening to a house
made of skin and bone.

I remember living
when I was a child,
playing in my mother's house,
toys scattered on the floor
next to the chair and desk,
or near the window,
and mother calling me
under the exposed light.

I'm a passage
through which I,
the one I was before,
walked, wanting warmth,

the small feeling
of pushing the door open
and looking past it,
alone.

You Made Me Think of Buchenwald

For Paul Victor

I can't sleep
in this small room anymore.

I want back everything I lost:
my wife, my family, my heart.

All this goes on inside,
and still, I'm a stranger
in my own house.

Who ever wanted this?
Not in real life.

My Life as a Hidden Child

For Jeannine Burk

First it was the earth.

Next came the various protozoa,
bacillus-ridden mud,
the amoeba
procreating indefinitely.

Then a birch tree
leaning into the wind
like a fluttering paper sack.

Then some insects
burrowed in its bark:
a cockroach,
a gadfly,
a fire ant.

Next, it was the goat,
which walked on four legs.

Then some men and some more.

And when there were enough men,
some of them discussed and decided
to commit one man to science
and philosophy and sliced his throat
five times to get to the blood
and the bone and the soul.

They found the heart—
hard and sticking out
like a knife
from the center of the body.
They questioned it
and broke it into pieces.
Out of the pieces came woman.
Everyone was scared.
Next, man jabbed a hook
into her neck and hung her
from the ceiling.

From the cut skin
another body was born.

Out of this came the child:
sliding out of the small slit,
falling to the floor like a leaf,
wet and crying in the light.

Finally, there were three—
Man, Woman, Child,
and the lost dead.

Solitary Confinement Changed Me

for Brian Nelson

I'm back in that cell,

a box of death,
and sometimes love:

generations of spiders
growing in front of me
is what I need
to keep me
to the living.

Once, I tried to rescue a moth
by stitching together
its broken wing
with a strand of my own hair.

A full year passes,
and no escape from the corner
I've made my own.

At the edge
of the courtyard,
nothing stands behind me.

Warsaw

Warsaw arrived in search of me.

I don't know how,
or why,
or when.

Some streets curve toward Białołęka.
Some lead to Łomza
or Bemowo.

I can say a few words: *Jestem, jeden, dwa.*
It's difficult to get through
to you, love.

When I'm alone,
far away from you,
I say the words in Polish:
I love you, *Kocham cie.*

Kocham cie, Warsaw.
Even if you do not.

Do Widzenia: Goodbye

Tomorrow you'll be in another country.

I don't know if the moon sleeps there,
and if it will divide you between here
or there, yes or no,
stay or go.

You'll want it to leave you alone
and you'll want it to stay,
to say your name before mine.

You'll try to sleep,
but you'll think of the place you were born,

your dead mother,
your drunk father,
your uncles.

The moon will show you its face,
make you remember
when I read you Lorca:

This is for you,
this opening.

V

Amsterdam Love

I imagine you in Amsterdam,
walking on its locomotive streets
glazed with yogurt,
glazed with lost loves,

with rusty, treadless poems,

the ones I gave you
and you never read.
I still hope you read them
and they will stick to the inside of your thighs
like the meat of an avocado
to its shell.

You won't notice
this torn America,

this gnarled highway,
these enumerations, split

inside my head.

You won't remember
the machinery of love.

You will only think of my face
in the light,

reflecting you.

Last Night I Had a Crazy Dream about You

We were in Italy.

I was talking to a woman that was familiar,
but I never saw her before.

I told her I remembered
a street musician playing a song
for three days.

I can't remember the song,
but I told her how
it reminded me of you,
how I cried every day he played.

We walked over a bridge.

I miss you.
You were with me in my dream
walking with me,
but I couldn't see
or touch you.

I wanted you so much
and I couldn't have you.

I couldn't speak,
but the song lit the center
inside me.

The Small Room on an Island

For Sebo

I live on an island in a small room.

In the morning, I count the boats on the sea.
I give them each a name.

I'm reading Empedocles.
He says, at one time, all the limbs,
which are the body's portions,
are brought together by Love.

Even though you may not be able to walk,
your heart walks in your heart.

There are times when I wake,
and I look at my legs.

I can walk and run.

Why do we look at the body
as a vision of paradise?

I'm not sure if I'll get off this island
in time to sit in bed with you.

The land stretches to forever.

And I can't, somehow, describe
a very simple feeling.

Everything will be all right,

the way it was
in the beginning.

At Fifteen

I measured time in cigarettes.
Underneath the underpass
I popped reds
and dropped blues
next to sucked off Popsicle sticks.
I straddled the concrete curb
and anointed the night with love.
I was alive—
snorting coke in abandoned homes
where pigeon shit painted the floor white.
I ripped off loose wood and climbed
to the top of the roof.
I wanted to feel the air
against my cheeks and fuck.
I wanted to break in half.
Fold like heaven and hell.
I was at war with myself.
At fifteen, I hummed paradise,
became those streets that tied
into other streets,
became my own country.
How I talked.
I could've been anyone.
I was incurable.

At Seventeen

I'm not powerless.
I'm just caught
in the wreckage of my age,
crouched in the eye
of getting high in the middle of small
and big town, USA,
with no place to go,
my face buried in the *War of Art*,
a fundamentalist,
an artist,
free and young,
drowning in optimism
and fast cars
and fingering,
sucking on the ideals
of some boy's promise
that they'll take me home tonight,
carry me over their shoulder
while I'm drunk and defeated
and turned down by sin,
governed by no one,
condemned to creating
a better world.

Moving On

I go on living
as if I were the world's
only daughter.

At night, I find myself
thirty miles down my body
searching for forgiveness.

I want to believe
there is freedom in acceptance.

What would my angels say?

Now that I've been served,
caught in the sleeplessness of my penance,
the anger of it all.

God, give me strength
so that I may do all things.

Dear Heart

Why do you pump harder-harder
when I think of the future?

I hear the faint blast
of air

when I hold you
to my ear.

The necessary repetition

reminds me

of my thoughts
my thoughts

oh heart,
dear heart

my thoughts.

This Is Why I Wrote This

There is no hope for love.

What are we trying to do?
When I see you there,
I want all of you,

even if you're raw
and stripped
of questions.

I walk with nothing in my hands,
but a feeling.

There is nothing else left.

Where Can We Go from Here?

It's still raining outside.

I want to leap out the window
and let the rain catch me
in its wet grief.

I hate the page,
especially when the poem is fucked.

Still, I must write this alone.

On Memory and Forgetting

I've spent my life knowing nothing.

I'd like to be able to remember
my body in the world,
before I forgot
its direct correspondence within it.

I want to be one of those people
having a good time somewhere.
I'd like to remember my body in the world.

I want to be one of those people, somewhere,
having a good time,
and remember my name before it was broken,
all its particulars,
its small catastrophes.

In the absence of place
and with the help of medicine,

I hope I can feel again.

My memories don't believe
their own stories,

don't remember my body in the world,
or even the name
of the place I was born
without medicine.

I'm not sure how to come back,
if I'll come back.

Only Human

Try being human
he said,

and figure out what
you want to say.

Get it half-written,
and type as if you had your hands
for one more hour,

as if they would be sold
across towns and labyrinths
and you never see your hands again.

Think about what you'd write
in the last hour you had your hands.

Write about losing your hands to writing,
then regaining them
in a battle for your hands,

the fight
to take back your hands,
to make them yours again,
and fold them together.

Hold your hand
in your other hand,
then point to yourself.

Hold your hands to your head
in the shape of a gun.

Hold yourself with your hands,
and lean on your hands.

Keep the hands moving
in the same direction,

hold,
hug,
and fight back.

Write the story
for your hands
by your hands,

and sit up,

let the hands
wipe away the tears,

and lift
the body up.

Then wipe the palm clean,
start something new,
the truth.

Think
what it would be like

to write something new
with these hands,

all the words in the right order.

The Living

We speak of living
not dying.

Of the roses
in the backyard,
the time we made love
in the abandoned parking lot
on the gravel floor,
and of the sadness
that came when we moved
far off
to other states,
then countries.

The last remaining
memories of our skin
turned into clothing
to keep us warm
in that secret place,
speaking that secret language.

In the dark we held out
our arms and talked
about the first time
we kissed at twenty
with the world slowing
down ahead of us,
and you going down
on me and sometimes
underneath the overpass,

the concrete ceiling
echoing with the roar
of cars and us talking,
breathing,
moving tongues
inside a cavernous place.

Is this what it's like to live
he asks.
Then I want wings.

I Fell In Love Again

I fell in love again
under the lightness of your skin,
shrouded myself
in the wetness of your lips
and kissed the beating heart
of your brain.

In the breath
is where the words are spoken.

I watch you sleep,
curled on the right side of the bed.

You speak in the small silence
where our backs touch.

I've made mistakes,
and I've cried for them
and wanted them to go away
deep, deep.

You're not a mistake, my love.

When I look at you, *all things go,*
all things go
like in the song "Chicago" I'm listening to
when I write this for you.

In bed we talk about planting
organic gardens,
and laugh like little children under covers,
playing with our bodies.

You're a train I want to ride all night.
I don't care where it's going.

Who can really figure out why
two people want each other?

All I know is there are no rules,
ever.

I think about the moment
I saw you dazed in sex fog,
the moment you came inside me, scared.

I lay awake at night, thinking
of your face over mine.

I walk with you in my heart
and backwards
with you in my heart
deep, deep.

So stop reading this.

Stop thinking about
why I write for you.

Stop thinking about when
your real life begins.

You, my train
I'll never get off.

Fall into the waves.

I Don't Want to Die

You walked me home in the rain,
water shoveling us
through the street
like scooped ice cream,

and then you nibbled on my arm,
poured sugar on the wound,
and applied your tongue
like a Band-Aid.

I'll Never Leave You

Did you ever love me?

I lived inside your lung once,
a blue bird
in your fleshy nest.
You took care of me.

How did you hold me? Remind me.

I pressed my face against
the cool glass of the window
and howled
as you walked past.

And then—

And then I walked naked
along the empty streets
while everyone was asleep

and we met in the middle
of our neighbor's front lawn,
our kisses curling up the grass.

Why did you go away?

I wrote you a poem
with lipstick.

My lips stained
the last stanza.

We Still Have Time

In the heart's open road,
in the suicide shotgun,

we'll work out our differences
and insecurities.

We'll become visitors
to our own images.

Sick, we'll vomit
dead hearts in our veins,
and forgive each other.

We'll be reborn
in the bend of each other's hands,
fertile and new.

There will be nothing left to talk about
but love.

Acknowledgements

The author wishes to acknowledge the editors of the following magazines, anthologies, and journals where these poems originally appeared:

Off Line: An Anthology of New Jersey Poets: "The Soul"

Nimrod International Journal: "The School with No Name"

Rutherford Red Wheelbarrow Poets Anthology: "Warsaw" and "Łomza"

Brink: "Warsaw"

The Aesthetica Creative Works Annual 2009: A version of "Remembering My Grandmother" originally titled "Carciofola"

Pablo Neruda/Hardman Poetry Prize finalist, Nimrod International Journal 2004: A version of "Remembering My Grandmother" originally titled "Carciofola"

Notes

Opening Epigraph: "I want/my heart back/I want to feel everything again" by Louise Glück from the poem "Blue Rotunda" in *Averno*.

The Devil's Breath: ". . . very dark, very hidden" adapted from the poem "Fugue" in *Averno* by Louise Glück.

I Fell in Love Again: ". . . all things go/all things go" and "I Fell in Love Again" are references from the song "Chicago" by Sufjan Stevens.

If I Were to Write a Suicide Note I Would Tell You: "The plums in the ice box have not made me want/to eat them more" is a reference to William Carlos Williams's poem "This is Just to Say."

McGraw-Hill published *Man's Concern With Death* by historian Arnold Toynbee in June 1969. Toynbee includes contributions from top ranking scholars and explores attitudes towards death, including what it may or may not be.

Łomza: Łomza is a city in North-Eastern Poland, approximately 90 miles from Warsaw.

Good Sleeping Weather: ". . . All the constituents of being are transitory. Work out your salvation with diligence." This was the last word of the Tathagata. Buddhism. Digha Nikaya ii.155-56, Mahaparinibbana Suttanta.

Ghosts in Love: A pastiche is a work that closely imitates the work of another poet. Phrasing inspired by the poem "Ghosts" by Julia Hartwig, Polish poet.

My God: Opening stanza from Yoruba poetry. Uli Beuer, *Yoruba Poetry: An Anthology of Traditional Poems.* (NY: Harry Abrams).

They Want You to Believe it Never Happened in the Ponary Forest: The poem refers to the Ponary massacre in the Ponary Forest where 70,000 Jews were shot by Nazi death squads and dumped into a pit. Ponary is 3.7 miles from Vilna, Lithuania.

The School with No Name: The poem references the Beslan school hostage crisis, which is also known as the Beslan school siege or Beslan massacre. The crisis took place in September 2004 and lasted three days. Islamic separatist militants, mostly Ingush and Chechen, occupied School Number One (SNO) in the town of Beslan, North Ossetia, and held 1,100 people hostage, including 777 children. Out of the 380 people killed, 186 were children.

"pulling the note from the lunch bag, /which began, 'Dear firefly,'" quoted from the poem "Words for Worry" in *Book of My Nights* (BOA Editions, 2001) by Li-Young Lee.

Solitary Confinement Changed Me: The article "Inside the Horrors of Solitary Confinement" by Jeff Tietz, originally published in *Rolling Stone*, issue 1171, December 6, 2012, inspires some phrasing in the poem.

You Made Me Think of Buchenwald: "One of the major Nazi concentration camps was set up in 1937 at Buchenwald, on the Ettersberg Hill near Weimar in Thüringen. Buchenwald remained one of the major camps throughout the history of the Third Reich, with numerous sub-camps under its administration. Buchenwald was not, *per se*, an extermination camp (such as Auschwitz), but prisoners were starved, maltreated, and worked to death in the camp quarry and adjacent armaments factories. Russian POWs and others were executed and cremated." (Geoff Walden, *The Third Reich in Ruins*)

My Life as a Hidden Child: Poem alludes to the story of Holocaust survivor Jeannine Burk who hid in a woman's house from age three to five, away from the Nazis during World War II.

Warsaw: Some phrasing inspired by the poem "Poetry" by Pablo Neruda. Writing to You, Forever and Ever: Jack and Ina Polak's love story appeared in an article "Love at First Sight, Transcending Nazi Internment" by Winter Miller posted on *The New York Times* website on December 5, 2007. The article tells the story of Jack and Ina Polak, two people who "found love in a concentration camp during World War II even though Jack was married to another woman at the time" (Miller). The love letters they wrote to each other inspired the poem.

About the Author

Photo By: Gerardo J Vitale

Loren Kleinman is a young, American-born poet with roots in New Jersey. Her poetry explores the results of love and loss, and how both themes affect an individual's internal and external voice. Loren has a BA in English Literature from Drew University and an MA in Creative and Critical Writing from the University of Sussex (UK). She was the recipient of the Spire Press Poetry Prize (2003), was a 2000 and 2003 Pushcart Prize nominee, and was a 2004 Nimrod/Pablo Neruda Prize finalist for poetry. Loren is also a columnist for IndieReader.com where she interviews *New York Times* bestselling indie authors.

CPSIA information can be obtained at www.ICGtesting.com
Printed in the USA
BVOW07s1742260814

364260BV00001B/8/P